Liberating Tamar
A Journey Toward Emotional Freedom
Workbook

Leontine S. Osuagwu

ISBN:1534809856
ISBN-13: 978-1534809857

DEDICATION

I dedicate this book and the accompanying workbook to my husband Emeka Osuagwu and to my children Joshua and Victoria who supported me through the formation of Liberating Tamar Inc., the writing of this book, and the accompanying workbook. I would not be where I am today in my journey of emotional wholeness without their love and support.

I also dedicate this work to my pastor, Dr. Dharius Daniels, Senior Pastor of Kingdom Church who took a leap of faith and allowed me to pilot this teaching with the women of his congregation in 2013. I will be forever grateful for his great teaching and exceptional leadership.

I would also like to thank some of the greatest women in my life namely Dr. Sharon Biggs, Wendy Reid, Valerie Mason-Chase and Lisa Hopkins for their support in helping bring this book and workbook project to completion. I love you ladies.

LEONTINE S. OSUAGWU

TABLE OF CONTENTS

FOREWORD

The message of this book is about liberating the TAMARs of the world – women stagnated within the receptacles of their own personal struggles and unsure of what steps they can take to become free.

Readers will find that the author, Leontine Osuagwu, speaks with a deliberate confidence generated largely by her own journey beyond suffering and onto survival after years of abuse. She emphasizes that women carrying emotional baggage from any type of TAMAR experience can do what she did: reclaim and reinvent themselves so they can live emotionally healed, freed, healthy and purpose-filled lives.

The author gives strategies TAMAR can easily put into practice during her quest for emotional healing. Her explanations about "The Liberation/TAMAR Process" describe the two-fold healing process where TAMAR first reaches deep within herself to allow her broken heart to be healed; and then reaches outside of herself so that others who have survived struggles can help triage any remaining wounds.

The truths embedded within each crevice of the book and its accompanying workbook acknowledge the fact that trauma, abuse, misunderstanding and rejection (TAMAR) can happen to any person at any time, yet, by applying the practical teachings in the book wholesome lives of liberation are attainable.

This book is for anyone journeying to be emotionally whole after experiencing any kind of TAMAR life experience. Leontine Osuagwu's experiences and perspective helps shape the book, and a review of the table of contents shows the depth and height of her message. The book will inspire, motivate and empower readers to reflect, and then process through healing so they can be free to experience the fullness of what life has for them.

> —Dr. Sharon M. Biggs, Executive Leadership Coach
>
> Co-author of *The DNA of Gutsy Leaders*©
>
> and Author of *The Silo Effect*©

MY STORY, THE VISION

My name is Leontine Osuagwu. In 2008, God gave me an assignment to the body of Christ called "Liberating Tamar Inc.". Liberating Tamar Inc. specializes in ministering healing to women who carry emotional baggage as a result of all kinds of abuse (physical, emotional, mental and psychological). We teach women how to reclaim their identity, their self-esteem, their confidence and ultimately their freedom through the word of God, the ministry of the Holy Spirit and the power of prayer.

This ministry was birthed out of my own struggles with rejection, low self-esteem, anger, and self-hatred after being sexually abused as a child between the ages of 3 and 6 years old. I was also emotionally and physically abused as a young adult which compounded my emotional issues.

The name of the ministry is inspired by the story of Tamar in the Bible in **2 Samuel 13**. Tamar was King David's only daughter. King David who was the second king of Israel, had eight wives, multiple concubines, nineteen sons and one daughter (**1 Chronicles 3**).

Tamar's story like so many stories across the globe is a story of deception, betrayal and violation. Tamar was raped by Amnon, her half-brother. Amnon fell in love with her and decided with the evil counsel of his friend Jonadab, to lure her into his tent and rape her (**2 Samuel 13:5**).

The story of Tamar is also a story of rejection. In **2 Samuel 13:15** the Bible states that after Amnon violated Tamar, he hated her exceedingly, so much so that the hatred with which he hated her was greater than the love with which he had loved her. As a result, he threw her out of his tent after satisfying his greedy lust.

Tamar's story is also one of mourning and emotional death. **2 Samuel 13:19** further states that Tamar put ashes on her head. This is symbolic of the mourning of a death. In Tamar's eyes, being stripped of her virginity and being rejected were equivalent to physical death. Not only was her innocence stolen, but her joy, her confidence, and her hope of ever being married were also destroyed.

Last but not least, it's also a story of despair and hopelessness. According to **2 Samuel 13:20**, Tamar remained desolate in her brother Absalom's house. When I read this verse, it terrified me because I realized that my life could have ended up in the same way. The enemy aborted her future by that one act of rape. The children that she was destined to give birth to were never conceived. The husband that she was to marry never got to meet her. The career, ministry or family that she was to start, never came to fruition. She never fulfilled God's plan for her life because she remained stuck in that season of her life.

Liberating Tamar's mandate is to ensure that women who experience physical and emotional abuse do not share TAMAR's fate. Liberating Tamar is more about fixing the emotional dysfunction in women's lives than it is about any "specific trauma" so even though you may not have experienced sexual molestation, you can still benefit from this book and from the accompanying study.

God has given us a couple of acronyms for TAMAR. The first one is **"Traumatized, Abused, Misunderstood and Rejected"**. If you've ever been through anything that has left you feeling traumatized, abused, misunderstood and rejected, Liberating TAMAR can help you.

Traumatized

The word traumatized means "to be in shock". In other words, you are emotionally stuck and can't seem to shake the shame, condemnation, unforgiveness etc.....

You may not have been sexually molested but your father may have left you and your mother, causing you to experience feelings of rejection and abandonment. As a result of these feelings, you now struggle with commitment in relationships for fear of being abandoned or rejected.

Another scenario may be that your husband may have left you for another woman and somehow the enemy has made you believe that you are the reason why he left thereby plaguing you with guilt, shame and condemnation. This teaching is for you!

Abused

The word abuse is defined as "utilizing something or someone in a way that is contrary to their purpose".

A woman's purpose is to:

Be loved: **Ephesians 5:25** states that husbands should love their wives as Christ loved the church and gave Himself for her.

Be a helper: God tells us in **Genesis 2:18** that because it is not good for a man to be alone, He will make him a helper that is suitable for him. The woman is that suitable helper.

Birth and Nurture: **Genesis 3** states that the woman shall give birth. **Isaiah 49:15** talks about a woman who cannot forget her nursing child and who will always have compassion on the son of her womb which speaks to her nurturing nature.

Anything that causes a woman to feel unloved is abuse and anything that challenges a woman's ability to be the birther, helper, and, nurturer that God has called her to be is abuse. If your husband is committing adultery, he is abusing you because he is making you feel unloved. If your husband is not communicating openly with you and is not allowing you to have input into his decision making, he is abusing you because he is not allowing you to fulfill your purpose as his helper. This teaching is for you!

Misunderstood

Emotional dysfunction leads us to behave in ways that we don't want to behave which causes people to misunderstand our motives. Being mistreated and taken advantage of for a long time can lead to defensiveness and hyper-sensitivity which taints the lens through which see people and the way we process what people say to us. This teaching is for you!

Rejected

Rejection is the feeling of being dismissed because of a perceived inadequacy or unworthiness. For example: "They abused me because I am ugly." "They cheated on me because I am overweight." "They beat me because I nagged them." "They won't associate with me because I am not good enough." This teaching is for you!

Psalms 147:3 shows healing as a twofold process.

First, the internal component or the healing of the broken heart is done through the ministry of the word of God, the power of the Holy Spirit and prayer.

The second part of the healing process is the binding up of the wounds. Binding is the process of tightly securing with a cloth or bandage in order to protect the wound from further harm.

This binding requires skill in order to prevent further damage to the wound. I believe this type of attention and care can only be provided by someone who has walked in the same shoes as the wounded to whom they are ministering.

In addition to skilled and careful hands, binding requires the participation of the wounded. Binding cannot be effective without the willingness of the participant. This is demonstrated by their cooperation in what I call the *"Liberation /TAMAR Process"* which involves the following:

Truth: Women must accept the Truth of the word of God.

Assimilation: Women must assimilate the Truth that they have been exposed to.

Mentality: Women must change their thinking according to the word that they have assimilated.

Application: Women must act on the word that they have learned.

Rest: Women must rest in the confidence that God will finish what he started in their lives and provide the freedom that they need.

This book is broken down into twelve (12) chapters and can be read on its own or can be studied with the corresponding workbook within the context of a Bible study. Please note that all scriptures are taken from the New King James Version (NKJV) of the Bible unless otherwise noted. **Ephesians 1:3** states that we have been blessed with all spiritual blessings in heavenly places in Christ Jesus and these blessings include our emotional freedom. I believe that as you read this book and apply the teachings to your life, liberation can become a reality.

God bless you and let's embark on this new journey toward emotional liberation.

Leontine Osuagwu
Founder/CEO of Liberating Tamar Inc.
www.LiberatingTamar.org

CHAPTER 1:

TRAUMA HAPPENS!

---

2 Samuel 13:20 c

So Tamar remained and was desolate in her brother Absalom's house.

Objectives

➤ Each woman will introduce herself and share with others what she expects to get out of the class.

➤ Discuss the importance of acknowledging where we are and the impact of the trauma on our life (emotionally, physically, mentally, relationally and financially).

➤ We will identify some of the consequences and baggage associated with physical and emotional abuse.

➤ We will explain from a biblical perspective why we do not have to remain stuck like TAMAR.

Activity 1:

❖ What does the Bible say about the nature of God as it relates to evil?

❖ Why do bad things happen to good people?

❖ How does the answer to the previous question change your perspective on your story?

❖ Emotional wholeness assessment

This activity must be done individually. After completion, total the scores and share with the class:

X <=45	45> X <60	X =>60
There's work to do	You are emotionally stable but you can improve	Any improvement is gravy

Circle the number that reflects your emotional condition in each of the below instances (1 being the least true and 5 being the truest).

Example: I often get impatient   1   2   3   4   5

No way   Absolutely

1. I've never felt betrayed   1   2   3   4   5
2. I've never felt taken advantage of 1   2   3   4   5
3. I always feel confident   1   2   3   4   5
4. I always feel intelligent   1   2   3   4   5
5. I never feel lonely   1   2   3   4   5
6. I've always felt attractive   1   2   3   4   5
7. I always feel loved   1   2   3   4   5
8. I always feel appreciated   1   2   3   4   5
9. I love being me   1   2   3   4   5
10. I always feel adequate   1   2   3   4   5
11. I always feel accepted   1   2   3   4   5

12. I have nothing to hide	1	2	3	4	5
13. I am not afraid of failure	1	2	3	4	5
14. I am not afraid of success	1	2	3	4	5
15. I feel emotionally strong	1	2	3	4	5

Additional Notes:

<u>Activity 2</u>:

❖ How can **Philippians 3:13** help you make a change in your life?

❖ Perform the following activity in small groups and take turns answering the questions.

    a. What would you change about yourself or about your life if you had a miracle potion?

b. What is the most traumatic experience in your life and how has it impacted you?

Activity 3:

Have you ever felt stuck? Explain.

Activity 4:

❖ Why do you think people hold on to relationships that are destructive to them? Share from your personal experience.

❖ From your perspective, based on Jeremiah 33:3 what are some of the "great and mighty" things that you would like God to reveal to you?

Activity 5:

❖ How have you fought God's process in your life? Please explain.

❖ **Psalm 46:10**-"Cease striving and know that I am God; I will be exalted among the nations, I will be exalted in the earth." (New American Standard Bible)

What does "striving" refer to in **Psalms 46:10** how can striving hurt our liberation process?

Trusting God Accepting Myself and Rising
(TAMAR)

Trusting God:

How will your trust in God change going forward as a result of this lesson?

Accepting Myself:

In which main area will you be more patient with yourself?

Rising:

What main step will you take in order to move forward?

NOTES:

NOTES:

CHAPTER 2

THE LOVING PHYSICIAN

Psalms 147:3

He heals the broken in heart, and binds up their wounds.

Objectives

➢ Settle once and for all that God is love and that He is not the author of the evil that has happened to us (**Romans 8:31-39**).

➢ Determine that God is the good physician (**Psalms 147:3**) and that we must partner with Him in our journey toward emotional freedom (**Isaiah 1:19**).

<u>Activity 1</u>

❖ Why do you think surrendering to God is such an important part of the healing process?

❖ What area in your life have you not surrendered to God and why?

Activity 2

❖ Have you ever blamed God for anything that has happened to you? Please explain.

❖ How do you reconcile **Psalms 92:15** with what you have gone through in your life?

❖ Do you know with absolute certainty that God loves you? If so why? If not, why?

Activity 3:

❖ What are some of the flaws (physical or otherwise) that you've had a hard time dealing with?

❖ How does **1 Corinthians 1:27** speak to your personally?

Activity 4:

❖ What part does God play in our liberation process?

❖ What part do we play in our liberation process?

Trusting God Accepting Myself and Rising
(TAMAR)

Trusting God:

How will your trust in God change going forward as a result of this lesson?

Accepting Myself:

In which main area will you be more patient with yourself?

Rising:

What main step will you take in order to move forward?

NOTES

CHAPTER 3:

SCRAPING THE SURFACE

Proverbs 28:13

He who covers his sins will not prosper,
but whoever confesses and forsakes *them* will have mercy.

Objectives

➢ Stress the importance of being honest with yourself, God and others (**Proverbs 28:13**).

➢ Find out who God has ordained for us to be.

<u>Activity 1:</u>

❖ What part of your personality do you like the most? Why?

❖ What part of your personality do you like the least? Why? Do you believe God can help you with that?

Activity 2:

What does the story of the woman that was caught in adultery teach you about God (**John 8:1-11**)?

Activity 3:

❖ How has your need for acceptance caused you to behave in the past?

❖ Insecurity is an extreme sense of inadequacy. What are some of the struggles that you've had with insecurity?

Activity 4:

❖ What are some of the negative ways that you used to see yourself or still see yourself?

❖ Contrast what God has done in Jacob's life with what He is looking to do in your life as TAMAR.

Activity 5:

❖ Are you satisfied with your progress in life? If not, why not?

❖ What are some of your frustrations? Please explain

Trusting God Accepting Myself and Rising
(TAMAR)

Trusting God:

How will your trust in God change going forward as a result of this lesson?

Accepting Myself:

In which main area will you be more patient with yourself?

Rising:

What main step will you take in order to move forward?

NOTES

CHAPTER 4

MOVING PAST GUILT, SHAME AND CONDEMNATION

Romans 8:1 (KJV)

There is therefore now no condemnation to them which are in Christ Jesus, who walk not after the flesh, but after the Spirit.

Objectives

➢ Come to understand that the enemy uses guilt, shame and condemnation to hinder our destiny.

➢ Come to realize that freedom from guilt, shame and condemnation was provided as part of the atonement.

Activity 1:

❖ What are you the most guilty, ashamed of or condemned about?

❖ What does the Bible say about Condemnation in Romans 8:1?

Activity 2:

How has guilt, shame and condemnation impeded your progress in your marriage, your career and or your family?

Activity 3:

What are some of the things that you've blamed yourself for or are currently blaming yourself for and why?

Activity 4:

Genesis 19:24-26-Then the LORD rained down burning sulfur on Sodom and Gomorrah--from the LORD out of the heavens. Thus He overthrew those cities and the entire plain, destroying all those living in the cities--and also the vegetation in the land. But Lot's wife looked back, and she became a pillar of salt.

❖ What does this scripture tell us about regret?

❖ How can you relate to this passage?

Trusting God Accepting Myself and Rising
(TAMAR)

Trusting God:

How will your trust in God change going forward as a result of this lesson?

Accepting Myself:

In which main area will you be more patient with yourself?

Rising:

What main step will you take in order to move forward?

NOTES

NOTES

CHAPTER 5

THE GRACE OF FORGIVENESS

Matthew 18:21-22

Then came Peter to Him, and said, Lord, how often shall my brother sin against me, and I forgive him? till seven times? Jesus said to him, I do not say to you, up to seven times, but up to seventy times seven.

Objectives

➢ We will determine that forgiveness (receive forgiveness from God; forgive yourself, others and God) is not an option because God expects us to forgive over and over regardless of how many times we have been violated (**Matthew 18:22-23**).

➢ Determine that unforgiveness is a blessing blocker and opens the door to the enemy (**Matthew 18:21-35**).

Activity 1:

Tell us about a time where you held unforgiveness towards:
    a. Yourself

    b. Others

c.   God

Activity 2:

❖ Why is unforgiveness a sin? Back it up with scripture.

a. How do people justify holding unforgiveness?

Activity 3:

❖ Why is it important to confront situations (with God's direction) instead of pushing them under the rug? Provide a scripture reference.

❖ What are the 4 steps in the confrontation process? Where do you see an example of these in the Bible?

Activity 4:

Matthew 5:23-24 (New International Version)

Therefore, if you are offering your gift at the altar and there remember that your brother or sister has something against you, leave your gift there in front of the altar. First go and be reconciled to them; then come and offer your gift.

What does this scripture say about the impact that unresolved offense can have on your relationship with God?

Activity 3:

Luke 6:42-How can you say to your brother, 'Brother, let me take the speck out of your eye,' when you yourself fail to see the plank in your own eye? You hypocrite, first take the plank out of your eye, and then you will see clearly to remove the speck from your brother's eye.

a. How does this scripture relate to unforgiveness?

b. What have you been holding on to that's keeping you from fully experiencing the new life God has for you?

Trusting God Accepting Myself and Rising
(TAMAR)

Trusting God:

How will your trust in God change going forward as a result of this lesson?

Accepting Myself:

In which main area will you be more patient with yourself?

Rising:

What main step will you take in order to move forward?

NOTES

NOTES

CHAPTER 6:

SURVIVING BETRAYAL

Numbers 23:19 (NIV)

God is not human, that He should lie, not a human being, that He should change his mind. Does He speak and then not act? Does He promise and not fulfill?

Objectives:

➤ Define betrayal and establish that God is incapable of betrayal (**Numbers 29:19**).

➤ Understand that God has a plan even in betrayal.

➤ Outline steps on how to deal with betrayal.

Activity 1:

❖ Have you ever been betrayed? If so, how did it make you feel and how did you respond to the betrayal and/or the person who betrayed you?

❖ Psalm 55:12-16-If an enemy were insulting me, I could endure it; if a foe were rising against me, I could hide. But it is you, a man like myself, my companion, my close friend, with whom I once enjoyed sweet fellowship at the house of God, as we walked about among the worshipers. Let death take my enemies by surprise; let them go down alive to the realm of the dead, for evil finds lodging among them. As for me, I call to God, and the LORD saves me.

What does this passage teach us about King David?

Have you been able to forgive the person or persons who betrayed you? If not, why not?

Activity 2:

❖   What is God's perspective on betrayal? Reference **John 15:20; 2 Timothy 3:12** and **Romans 8:28.**

❖ What are the 4 steps that we need to take after betrayal (reference scripture if possible).

❖ How can we tie God's hands in the liberation process?

Trusting God Accepting Myself and Rising (TAMAR)

Trusting God:

How will your trust in God change going forward as a result of this lesson?

Accepting Myself:

In which main area will you be more patient with yourself?

Rising:

What main step will you take in order to move forward?

NOTES

NOTES

CHAPTER 7:

VICTORY OVER REJECTION

---

2 Samuel 13:15

Then Amnon hated her very much. He hated her more than he had loved her. He said to her, "Get up! Go away!"

Objectives

➢ Define rejection and identify causes and symptoms.

➢ Explain God's process for dealing with rejection

Activity 1:

❖   What are some of the causes and symptoms of rejection?

❖ Which symptoms of rejection have you struggled with or are you currently struggling with?

❖ What may be some of the causes of your personal struggles with rejection?

Activity 2:

❖ What does **Ephesians1:6** tell us about God's feeling about us? Why is it important for us to get that revelation?

❖ How can rejection destroy someone's future? Give an example of a biblical character who allowed rejection to destroy their life.

❖ Which practical steps can we take to get our deliverance from rejection? Which biblical character exemplifies this process?

Activity 3:

What is the best way to rest in God after we've been rejected?

Trusting God Accepting Myself and Rising
(TAMAR)

Trusting God:

How will your trust in God change going forward as a result of this lesson?

Accepting Myself:

In which main area will you be more patient with yourself?

Rising:

What main step will you take in order to move forward?

NOTES

NOTES

CHAPTER 8:

THERE'S A BLESSING IN DYING

Romans 8:13

For if you live according to the flesh you will die; but if by the Spirit you put to death the deeds of the body, you will live.

Objectives

➢ Define what it means to die to the flesh (**1Corinthians 15:31**), explain why God expects us to die to our flesh and how to die to the flesh.

➢ Explain the blessings of humility and submission to God (**James 4:7 and 4:10**).

Activity 1:

❖ What does it mean to die to the flesh?

❖ How can yielding to the flesh, rob us of God's best? Use scripture.

❖ List 2 reasons why we need to die to the flesh? Explain.

1.--

2.--

Activity 2:

What are the 2 main ways to kill the flesh? Use scripture to explain.

1.--

2.--

Activity

What are the 3 main steps of emotional journaling?

    1.   --

    2.   --

    3.   --

Trusting God Accepting Myself and Rising
(TAMAR)

Trusting God:

How will your trust in God change going forward as a result of this lesson?

Accepting Myself:

In which main area will you be more patient with yourself?

Rising:

What main step will you take in order to move forward?

NOTES

NOTES

CHAPTER 9:

HOPE IN THE MIDST OF HOPELESSNESS

Psalms 118:17

I will not die but live, and will proclaim what the LORD has done.

Objectives:

➢ Understand that there's hope even in the worst if situations.

➢ Determine that Jesus paid the price for our peace.

➢ Determine that depression happens to many and that we are not alone.

➢ Understand that we have been equipped to fight depression.

Activity 1:

❖ What is the root of depression according to Proverb 12:25.

❖ What is the cure? Explain.

Activity 2:

List 3 symptoms of depression that you may have personally experienced.

1._____

2._____

3._____

Activity 3:

❖ As Christians, we do not have to put up with depression. Why? Use Isaiah 53:5 and Colossians 2:15.

❖ List the names of 2 biblical characters who battled depression. Explain using scripture.

1._____

2._____

❖ How does it make you feel to know that chosen men of God have also struggled with depression?

Activity 4:

List 3 weapons that we have been equipped with to defeat depression.

1._____

2._____

3._____

Activity 5

How can we be grateful when we are going through a storm ? Use scripture.

Trusting God Accepting Myself and Rising
(TAMAR)

Trusting God:

How will your trust in God change going forward as a result of this lesson?

Accepting Myself:

In which main area will you be more patient with yourself?

Rising:

What main step will you take in order to move forward?

NOTES

CHAPTER 10:

CONQUERING LOW SELF-ESTEEM

Psalms 139:14

I praise You because I am fearfully and wonderfully made; Your works are wonderful, I know that full well.

Objectives

➢ Define self-esteem and identify the causes and symptoms.

➢ Determine that God does not want us to remain plagued with low self-esteem.

➢ Learn to define our sense of worth based on the Word of God

Activity 1:

❖ What are some of the causes and symptoms of low self-esteem?

❖ Which symptoms of low self-esteem have you struggled with or are you currently struggling with?

❖ How have these symptoms affected your relationships?

Activity 2:

❖ Low self-esteem causes us to view ourselves as insignificant and can rob us of our destiny.

From your personal experience, is there something that you feel that you've lost as a result of low self-esteem? Please explain.

❖ Give an example of how a person or persons missed their destiny because of low self-esteem (**Numbers 13**).

Activity 3:

❖ Low self-esteem causes us to make excuses.
Give examples of biblical characters who made excuses as a result of their low self-esteem. Reference scripture (**Exodus 3:11-12; Judges 6:15-16**).

❖ Share from your personal experience any excuses you've made as a result of low self-esteem.

Activity 4:

❖ What should be our focus when we feel plagued by low self-esteem? Provide a scripture reference.

❖ What are some of the reasons why it should be easy for us to accept ourselves (**John 3:16; Genesis1:27; Ephesians 2:10; Psalms 139:14**)?

Trusting God Accepting Myself and Rising
(TAMAR)

Trusting God:

How will your trust in God change going forward as a result of this lesson?

Accepting Myself:

In which main area will you be more patient with yourself?

Rising:

What main step will you take in order to move forward?

NOTES

CHAPTER 11:

THE SECURITY OF "LETTING GO"

---

1 Peter 5:7

Casting all your care upon Him; for He cares for you.

Objective

- Explain why trust is required for surrender to take place.

- Define what it means to surrender to God (**Psalms 46:10**) and to the Holy Spirit.

- Identify the steps that we need to take in order to surrender.

Activity 1:

❖ What does it mean to surrender?

❖ What are 3 of the main areas in your life that God has been asking you to surrender to Him? What was your response and why?

     1. _____

2. _____

3. _____

Activity 2:

❖ List 2 benefits of surrender using scripture.

  a. --

  b. --

❖ What must come first before surrender can take place?

❖ Why is it so hard for some of us to trust God with our emotions? Explain using an example from your personal experience.

❖ How can our refusal to surrender impact our lives?

Activity 3:

What are the 3 steps that we need to take before we can fully trust God? (use scripture reference)

  o Step 1:

  o Step 2:

  o Step 3

Trusting God Accepting Myself and Rising
(TAMAR)

Trusting God:

How will your trust in God change going forward as a result of this lesson?

Accepting Myself:

In which main area will you be more patient with yourself?

Rising:

What main step will you take in order to move forward?

NOTES

NOTES

CHAPTER 12

FINDING PURPOSE

Luke 22:31-32

And the Lord said, "Simon, Simon! Indeed, Satan has asked for you, that he may sift *you* as wheat. But I have prayed for you; that your faith should not fail; and when you have returned to *Me*, strengthen your brethren."

Objectives

➤ Discover that God has a perfect plan for your life despite your narrative (**Jeremiah 29:11** and **Ephesians 2:10**).

➤ Determine that God does not waste your pain (**Genesis 50:20**) and that He intends to use it to benefit others (**Luke 22:32**).

Activity 1:

❖ What did Jesus pray specifically for Peter about? Why did He pray this type of prayer? Use scripture in your response.

❖ Give an example on how your faith was able to carry you through a particular situation in your life.

Activity 2:

❖ What is every believer's responsibility once we have recovered from the aftermath of trauma? (Luke 22:32).

❖ How does the answer to the previous question speak to you personally?

Activity 3

❖ What are the 3 S's of a living sacrifice?

1 _____

2 _____

3 _____

❖ How does God want to use us?

What are the main 2 ways that He wants us to testify?

a. --

b. --

Trusting God Accepting Myself and Rising
(TAMAR)

Trusting God:

How will your trust in God change going forward as a result of this lesson?

Accepting Myself:

In which main area will you be more patient with yourself?

Rising:

What main step will you take in order to move forward?

NOTES

NOTES

LAST THOUGHTS

This book is based on my personal liberation process. My faith in God and my personal relationship with Jesus Christ have not only allowed me to write this book and the accompanying workbook, but also to get to a point in my emotional journey where I am able to honestly say that my heart no longer reflects the pain and shame of my past. I am a living proof that God's liberation process works.

Congratulations on completing this study. It's a great tool that God can use to help you achieve emotional freedom. I must say however that a consistent demonstration of emotional stability and freedom cannot be reached unless you enter into a relationship with "The Liberator" Jesus Christ. The principles in the book and the activities in the workbook will help you get started in your liberation journey, but accepting Jesus Christ as your personal savior and Lord will give you the sustaining power to complete the journey. If you don't know the Lord Jesus Christ and would like to enter into a relationship with Him, please recite the following prayer out loud, trusting that God hears you:

Father, forgive me for my sins. Thank You for sending Your son Jesus to die on the cross and save my soul from eternal damnation. I receive Jesus' sacrifice today. Jesus, I want to be in relationship with You. Come into my heart and lead my life with peace and purpose. I accept You as Lord and savior. Amen!

You are now a part of the family of God. Ask Him to lead you to a Bible believing and Bible teaching church so you can grow in your faith. I encourage you to stay faithful to God, to His word and to His church as He continues to empower you to be all that He has created you to be. God has a great purpose for all of us and whatever the enemy has meant for evil in our lives, He has promised to turn into good. You are God's precious gem created in His image to accomplish a destiny that only you can fulfil and I cannot wait to hear about the many breakthroughs that will occur in your lives. I am tremendously excited and confident "in this very thing, that He which has begun a good work in you, will perform it until the day of Jesus Christ" (**Philippians 1:6**).

God bless

Leontine Osuagwu

Liberating Tamar Inc.

www.liberatingtamar.org

ABOUT THE AUTHOR

Leontine Osuagwu is a Bible Teacher with a passion to see every woman in the world emotionally whole and walking in their God ordained purpose. She is the founder and CEO of Liberating Tamar Inc., a 501C3 nonprofit organization mandated by God to help facilitate emotional freedom in the lives of survivors of physical and emotional abuse. Leontine Osuagwu is married to Emeka Osuagwu and they are the proud parents of Joshua and Victoria.

Made in the USA
Las Vegas, NV
01 September 2021